PRINCEWILL LAGANG

The Koch Chronicles: A Business Maverick's Journey to Influence and Impact

First published by PRINCEWILL LAGANG 2023

Copyright © 2023 by Princewill Lagang

All rights reserved. No part of this publication may be reproduced, stored or transmitted in any form or by any means, electronic, mechanical, photocopying, recording, scanning, or otherwise without written permission from the publisher. It is illegal to copy this book, post it to a website, or distribute it by any other means without permission.

Princewill Lagang asserts the moral right to be identified as the author of this work.

First edition

This book was professionally typeset on Reedsy. Find out more at reedsy.com

Contents

1	Introduction - Unveiling the Maverick's Odyssey	1
2	The Genesis of a Maverick	4
3	The Crucible of Innovation	6
4	The Nexus of Power and Politics	8
5	The Unraveling Tapestry	10
6	Resilience and Reinvention	12
7	Legacy Unveiled	14
8	Beyond the Chronicles	16
9	The Ever-Changing Horizon	18
10	Reflections and Continuations	20
11	Epilogue: The Everlasting Echo	22
12	The Unfinished Symphony	24
13	A Call to Action	26
14	Summary	28

1

Introduction - Unveiling the Maverick's Odyssey

In the heartland of America, where innovation meets ambition, the narrative of a business maverick unfolds—a narrative that traverses the corridors of power, challenges the status quo, and leaves an indelible mark on the landscape of American business and politics. "The Koch Chronicles: A Business Maverick's Journey to Influence and Impact" invites you on a compelling odyssey through the life, career, and enduring legacy of Charles Koch.

This chronicle is more than a recounting of corporate triumphs; it is a nuanced exploration of the complexities woven into the fabric of one of America's most influential entrepreneurs. From the early days of Koch Industries in the heart of Wichita, Kansas, to the corridors of power where political influence and business acumen converge, this narrative unveils the layers of Charles Koch's journey.

In this introduction, we set the stage for a captivating exploration of the Koch legacy. We navigate the genesis of Koch Industries, tracing the roots of a company that would grow to become one of the largest privately held conglomerates in the nation. As we embark on this journey, we delve into the formative years of Charles Koch, a visionary leader whose innovative spirit and commitment to principles would shape the trajectory of his career.

The narrative unfolds against the backdrop of a changing America, where economic shifts, technological advancements, and political upheavals set the stage for Charles Koch's ascent. From the early challenges of the oil and gas industry to the emergence of Koch Industries as a diversified powerhouse, we witness the strategic maneuvers and calculated risks that characterize the maverick's rise.

"The Koch Chronicles" is not merely a business biography; it is a tapestry that intertwines the worlds of business and politics. As Charles Koch becomes a central figure in political discourse, advocating for libertarian ideals and influencing policy discussions, we explore the intersection of ideology and corporate influence.

Amidst the triumphs, we confront the controversies and tensions that accompany such influence. The narrative pulls no punches in examining the internal dynamics of the Koch family, the scrutiny of business practices, and the complexities of navigating the intersection of corporate power and political engagement.

As we navigate through the chapters, each unveiling a new facet of Charles Koch's journey, the narrative evolves. It transcends a linear recounting of events and invites readers into a reflection on the broader implications of influence and impact. The story becomes not just a historical account but a living dialogue about the responsibilities of business leaders, the ethical dimensions of influence, and the ever-changing nature of legacy.

In "The Koch Chronicles," we embark on a journey that extends beyond the pages of a book—a journey that prompts readers to consider their roles in

INTRODUCTION - UNVEILING THE MAVERICK'S ODYSSEY

shaping the narratives of influence and impact in their own lives. Join us as we unveil the maverick's odyssey, exploring the enduring legacy of Charles Koch and the ripple effects that resonate through the tapestry of American history.

2

The Genesis of a Maverick

In the hushed corridors of Wichita, Kansas, where the prairie winds whisper tales of ambition, a legend was quietly taking shape. It was in this unassuming Midwestern town that our protagonist, Charles Koch, first embarked on a journey that would eventually redefine the landscape of American business. This is the genesis of a maverick, the opening chapter in "The Koch Chronicles: A Business Maverick's Journey to Influence and Impact."

The sun dipped low on the horizon as Charles, a young and eager entrepreneur with a visionary gleam in his eye, took his first steps into the world of business. The year was 1967, a time when the echoes of the Industrial Revolution still resonated through the hearts of aspiring capitalists. Armed with a degree in general engineering from the Massachusetts Institute of Technology and an insatiable appetite for innovation, Charles Koch was ready to make his mark.

This chapter delves deep into the Koch family's roots, tracing the lineage of industry pioneers and self-made tycoons whose stories became the foundation upon which Charles would build his own legacy. The reader is transported to the humble beginnings of the Koch empire, where Charles, alongside his brother David, laid the groundwork for what would become one of the most influential and controversial conglomerates in modern history.

As the narrative unfolds, we witness the birth of Koch Industries, a fledgling company in the heart of America that initially operated in the oil refining and chemicals sector. The challenges were formidable, the risks were high, but Charles Koch, a maverick in the making, embraced the turbulence of the business world with unyielding determination.

This chapter also explores the early influences that shaped Charles Koch's unique management philosophy. The reader is introduced to the guiding principles that would later be formalized as "Market-Based Management," a distinctive approach that blended free-market economics with organizational excellence. As the pages turn, the narrative paints a vivid picture of the trials, triumphs, and transformative moments that molded Charles into a business luminary.

Through meticulous research and intimate storytelling, "The Koch Chronicles" invites readers to witness the birth pangs of a business empire. From the fledgling days of Koch Industries to the emergence of Charles Koch as a thought leader in libertarian circles, this chapter sets the stage for a compelling odyssey—a journey of influence and impact that would leave an indelible mark on the American business landscape.

3

The Crucible of Innovation

In the sprawling landscape of the American heartland, where amber waves of grain meet the relentless march of progress, Charles Koch's journey continued to evolve. Chapter 2 of "The Koch Chronicles: A Business Maverick's Journey to Influence and Impact" brings to life a pivotal period in Koch Industries' trajectory, marked by innovation, risk-taking, and the relentless pursuit of excellence.

As the 1970s dawned, the energy crisis cast a long shadow over the United States, and the oil and gas industry found itself at the epicenter of a transformative storm. Against this backdrop, Charles Koch, armed with a visionary zeal, led Koch Industries into uncharted territory. This chapter unfolds against the backdrop of a crucible, where the fires of innovation and necessity forged the company's identity.

Readers are taken on a journey through the development of Koch Industries as it diversified its portfolio, venturing into new sectors such as pipelines, trading, and agriculture. The narrative illuminates the strategic decisions, calculated risks, and bold maneuvers that characterized Charles Koch's leadership during this pivotal era.

At the heart of the chapter lies the tale of Charles Koch's commitment to technological advancement and operational efficiency. The narrative explores how he fostered a culture of innovation within Koch Industries, empowering employees to think beyond conventional boundaries. Technological breakthroughs, automation, and a relentless pursuit of efficiency became the hallmarks of the company, setting it apart in an era defined by rapid change.

The reader is introduced to key figures within the Koch Industries family, each contributing their unique skills and perspectives to the company's growth. From engineers to entrepreneurs, this chapter weaves a tapestry of diverse talents converging under Charles Koch's leadership, shaping a corporate culture that prized intellectual curiosity and bold problem-solving.

As the narrative unfolds, readers witness the emergence of Charles Koch not only as a shrewd businessman but also as a champion of free-market principles. This chapter delves into the ideological underpinnings that would later become integral to the Koch brothers' influence on American politics. The seeds of libertarianism take root, as Charles Koch's commitment to limited government and individual freedom becomes increasingly intertwined with the corporate narrative.

"The Crucible of Innovation" is a chapter that encapsulates the transformative spirit of an era and the visionary leadership that propelled Koch Industries to the forefront of American business. It sets the stage for the subsequent chapters, where the intersection of business, ideology, and politics would converge in unexpected ways, ultimately shaping the legacy of a maverick and his enduring impact on the nation.

4

The Nexus of Power and Politics

As the wheels of innovation turned within Koch Industries, Charles Koch's journey took an unexpected turn, guiding him into the intricate web of power and politics. "The Koch Chronicles: A Business Maverick's Journey to Influence and Impact" continues with Chapter 3, exploring the nexus where corporate interests, ideology, and political ambitions converge.

The chapter unfolds against the backdrop of the late 1970s and early 1980s, a period marked by political upheaval and ideological fervor in the United States. Charles Koch, driven by a belief in limited government and free-market principles, recognized the potential for influencing policy to align with these ideals. This chapter delves into the genesis of Koch's foray into the political arena, marking a significant juncture in the evolution of his influence.

Readers are introduced to the establishment of think tanks and advocacy groups funded by Charles Koch, aimed at shaping public discourse and policy discussions. The narrative explores how these entities became vehicles for promoting libertarian ideals, influencing policymakers, and challenging the prevailing narrative on the role of government in society.

The chapter unravels the complex relationships forged by Charles Koch within political circles, as he navigates the corridors of power with a dual commitment to advancing his business interests and promoting a libertarian agenda. From campaign contributions to strategic alliances, the narrative peels back the layers of the political chessboard where Koch played a pivotal role.

As the Koch brothers' political activities gain momentum, the narrative examines the controversies and criticisms that accompany their ascent. The influence of Koch Industries in shaping policy debates, particularly in areas such as environmental regulation and taxation, becomes a focal point of discussion. The reader is presented with a nuanced exploration of the fine line between corporate advocacy and political influence.

"The Nexus of Power and Politics" also introduces readers to the tensions and alliances within the broader political landscape. The chapter examines Charles Koch's interactions with like-minded individuals and organizations, as well as the conflicts that arise with those who view his influence with skepticism. It paints a portrait of a man who, propelled by conviction, becomes a polarizing figure in both business and political spheres.

As the chapter unfolds, readers witness the emergence of the Koch brothers as formidable players in American politics, challenging the status quo and reshaping the political narrative. This intersection of power, ideology, and political maneuvering sets the stage for the chapters to come, where the impact of the Koch legacy extends far beyond the boardroom, leaving an indelible mark on the nation's political landscape.

5

The Unraveling Tapestry

"The Koch Chronicles: A Business Maverick's Journey to Influence and Impact" continues its narrative in Chapter 4, where the intricate tapestry of Charles Koch's life and legacy encounters both triumphs and tribulations. This chapter unravels the complexities of Koch Industries, the family dynamics, and the external forces that tested the resilience of the Koch legacy.

As the 1980s unfolded, Koch Industries, under Charles Koch's stewardship, became a corporate juggernaut, expanding its reach into various industries and solidifying its position as one of the largest privately held companies in the United States. The narrative explores the triumphs of this era, from strategic acquisitions to technological innovations, weaving a story of corporate success and ambition.

However, success did not shield the Koch family from internal challenges. The chapter delves into the dynamics between Charles and his brother David, exploring the tensions and collaborations that defined their relationship. As the brothers navigated the intricate landscape of family-owned enterprises, conflicting visions and differing approaches to business and politics came to the forefront.

Simultaneously, external forces began to shape the narrative. The regulatory landscape, economic fluctuations, and the ever-shifting dynamics of global markets became formidable challenges. The narrative unfolds against a backdrop of legal battles and public scrutiny, exploring how Koch Industries navigated controversies and adapted to the changing tides of public opinion.

This chapter also examines the evolution of Charles Koch's public persona. As the Koch name became synonymous with both corporate success and political controversy, Charles found himself in the spotlight. The narrative peels back the layers of the public image, exploring the challenges and responsibilities that accompanied his role as a business leader and political influencer.

Amidst the corporate and personal challenges, the chapter highlights Charles Koch's unwavering commitment to the principles that guided his journey. The reader witnesses the continuation of his engagement in political advocacy, philanthropy, and the promotion of libertarian ideals. The chapter paints a nuanced picture of a man whose convictions weathered the storms of public opinion and internal strife.

"The Unraveling Tapestry" sets the stage for the latter chapters of the chronicle, where the legacy of Charles Koch undergoes further transformations. As the narrative unfolds, readers are invited to witness the intricate interplay of family, business, and ideology, exploring how the threads of influence and impact are woven into the fabric of American history.

6

Resilience and Reinvention

In the ever-evolving saga of "The Koch Chronicles: A Business Maverick's Journey to Influence and Impact," Chapter 5 unveils a period of resilience and reinvention. Charles Koch, ever the strategic visionary, faced challenges head-on and forged a path that would leave an enduring mark on both business and society.

As the 1990s dawned, the landscape of American industry underwent seismic shifts. Globalization, technological advancements, and the dawn of the information age presented both opportunities and challenges. Charles Koch, recognizing the need for adaptability, steered Koch Industries through a process of reinvention.

This chapter explores the diversification strategies undertaken by Koch Industries during this era. From energy and commodities to finance and technology, the company's portfolio expanded, reflecting Charles Koch's keen foresight and ability to position the business for a rapidly changing world.

The narrative delves into the role of innovation in Koch Industries' resilience. Technological advancements, operational efficiencies, and a commitment to sustainability emerged as integral components of the company's ethos. The reader is immersed in the dynamic landscape where Koch Industries thrived by embracing change rather than resisting it.

Amidst this period of corporate evolution, the chapter also unravels the continued intertwining of business and politics in the Koch legacy. Charles Koch's advocacy for free-market principles and limited government found new avenues, influencing policy discussions and shaping public perception. The narrative explores the delicate balance between corporate interests and political influence, shedding light on the challenges and controversies that accompanied this dual role.

The personal dimensions of Charles Koch's life also come into focus in Chapter 5. The narrative examines the interplay between family dynamics, philanthropy, and the broader societal impact of the Koch name. As Charles Koch engaged in philanthropic endeavors and contributed to educational initiatives, the chapter explores the multifaceted dimensions of his legacy beyond the boardroom.

As the chapter unfolds, readers witness the resilience of Charles Koch and Koch Industries in the face of adversity. The company's ability to adapt, innovate, and reinvent itself reflects the maverick spirit that has characterized Charles Koch's journey. This chapter sets the stage for the concluding chapters of the chronicle, where the full scope of Charles Koch's influence and impact on business, politics, and society is laid bare.

7

Legacy Unveiled

In the final installment of "The Koch Chronicles: A Business Maverick's Journey to Influence and Impact," Chapter 6 unveils the culmination of Charles Koch's storied legacy—a legacy that transcends the boundaries of business, politics, and societal influence.

As the 21st century unfolds, the narrative follows Charles Koch into a chapter marked by reflection and a profound examination of the impact he has had on the world. The chapter delves into the evolution of Koch Industries into a global powerhouse, exploring its continued diversification, technological innovations, and contributions to economic landscapes around the world.

The intertwining of business and politics, a hallmark of Charles Koch's journey, is brought to its zenith in this chapter. Readers witness the enduring influence of Koch Industries on policy discussions, political ideologies, and the broader societal discourse. The narrative navigates through the complex web of advocacy, think tanks, and philanthropic initiatives, providing a nuanced understanding of Charles Koch's multifaceted approach to leaving a lasting imprint on the world.

The chapter also reflects on the personal dimensions of Charles Koch's legacy. The reader is invited to explore the intricate interplay between family, business, and the philanthropic endeavors that define the Koch name. As Charles Koch's children and successors step into prominent roles within Koch Industries, the narrative underscores the continuation of a legacy that extends beyond a single individual.

Philanthropy emerges as a central theme in this chapter, shedding light on the initiatives and causes that Charles Koch has championed. From educational endeavors to research institutions, the narrative paints a portrait of a man committed to the betterment of society, utilizing his wealth and influence for purposes that align with his vision for a freer and more prosperous world.

As the legacy of Charles Koch unfolds, the chapter navigates through the reflections of contemporaries, critics, and collaborators. The reader is presented with a comprehensive view of the impact of the Koch legacy on American business, politics, and society at large.

Ultimately, Chapter 6 serves as a culmination of the maverick's journey—a journey marked by resilience, reinvention, and a relentless pursuit of influence and impact. The legacy unveiled in these pages invites readers to contemplate the enduring contributions of Charles Koch, leaving them with a nuanced understanding of a business magnate whose influence resonates far beyond the boardroom.

8

Beyond the Chronicles

As "The Koch Chronicles: A Business Maverick's Journey to Influence and Impact" concludes, Chapter 7 takes readers beyond the confines of the narrative, exploring the enduring impact of Charles Koch's legacy on the business landscape, political discourse, and societal perspectives.

This chapter reflects on the ripple effects of Charles Koch's journey, transcending the boundaries of time and industry. It examines the ongoing influence of Koch Industries, now under the stewardship of successive generations, and how the company continues to navigate the complexities of a rapidly changing world.

The narrative expands to consider the broader implications of Charles Koch's influence on free-market principles and libertarian ideologies. Readers are prompted to reflect on the evolving role of corporations in shaping public policy and societal values, as well as the potential tensions between corporate interests and the public good.

The chapter explores the impact of the Koch brothers' political contributions and advocacy on the political landscape, prompting a nuanced discussion about the intersection of business and politics in the contemporary era. The reader is encouraged to consider the complexities of influence and power wielded by corporations in the democratic process.

Beyond the business and political spheres, the narrative delves into the philanthropic endeavors initiated by Charles Koch and his family. Readers are invited to contemplate the lasting contributions to education, research, and societal betterment that have become integral to the Koch legacy.

As the chapter unfolds, it invites readers to engage in a broader conversation about the role of business leaders in shaping the destiny of nations. The reader is prompted to consider questions about corporate responsibility, ethical leadership, and the balance between private enterprise and the public good.

In the concluding pages of Chapter 7, the narrative shifts towards the future. The reader is left to ponder the ongoing legacy of Charles Koch and Koch Industries, contemplating the trajectory of influence and impact in the years and decades to come. The story of Charles Koch, the business maverick, concludes not as a static chronicle but as a dynamic narrative with a lasting imprint on the American tapestry.

9

The Ever-Changing Horizon

In the final chapter of "The Koch Chronicles: A Business Maverick's Journey to Influence and Impact," the narrative turns its gaze towards the ever-changing horizon, acknowledging that legacies are not static, but rather dynamic entities influenced by the ongoing currents of time, society, and the business landscape.

As the story transitions into the contemporary era, the reader is immersed in the complexities of a world undergoing rapid transformation. Chapter 8 explores how Koch Industries adapts to emerging technologies, global challenges, and shifting consumer expectations. The narrative unveils the company's strategies for sustainability, innovation, and corporate responsibility, reflecting the evolving demands of a socially conscious and technologically driven society.

The chapter delves into the next chapters of the Koch legacy, examining how subsequent generations navigate the intricate balance between business stewardship, political engagement, and philanthropy. Readers witness the continuation of the Koch influence and impact, shaped by new voices, perspectives, and challenges.

THE EVER-CHANGING HORIZON

Beyond the corporate boardrooms, the narrative widens its lens to capture the broader implications of the Koch legacy on the discourse surrounding capitalism, individual liberty, and the role of corporations in society. The reader is prompted to reflect on the ongoing resonance of Charles Koch's principles in an era marked by debates about income inequality, corporate governance, and the ethical responsibilities of business leaders.

The chapter unfolds as a conversation about the future—an exploration of the possibilities, challenges, and responsibilities that lie ahead for Koch Industries and the legacy it carries. It invites readers to consider the role of business mavericks in shaping the destinies of nations and the ethical considerations that accompany such influence.

As the final pages turn, the narrative leaves room for contemplation. The reader is encouraged to envision the ever-changing horizon, recognizing that the legacy of Charles Koch is not a static endpoint but a continuum. It challenges readers to participate in the ongoing dialogue about the intersection of business, politics, and societal progress, understanding that the chapters yet to be written will shape the legacy in ways yet unforeseen.

Chapter 8 serves as a bridge from the chronicles of the past to the unwritten pages of the future, inviting readers to contribute to the narrative of influence and impact in their own ways. The legacy of Charles Koch, the business maverick, lives on not just in the pages of history but in the ongoing story of a world shaped by the forces of commerce, ideology, and the ever-changing horizon.

10

Reflections and Continuations

As "The Koch Chronicles: A Business Maverick's Journey to Influence and Impact" concludes, Chapter 9 invites readers to embark on a reflective journey, contemplating the enduring resonance of Charles Koch's legacy and its ripple effects across the landscapes of business, politics, and societal values.

This chapter serves as a collective reflection, weaving together the perspectives of historians, business analysts, and individuals influenced by the Koch legacy. The narrative delves into the complexities of assessing a multifaceted legacy, acknowledging both the accolades and criticisms that have accompanied Charles Koch's journey.

Readers are prompted to consider the evolving narratives surrounding Koch Industries and its impact on various industries, economies, and communities. The chapter explores how the company's practices, innovations, and corporate philosophies have contributed to the broader conversation about responsible business conduct in the 21st century.

Beyond the corporate realm, the narrative broadens its scope to examine the enduring influence of Charles Koch's political engagement. Readers are invited to explore the evolving dynamics of the intersection between business and politics, contemplating the implications for democratic processes, governance, and the role of private entities in shaping public policies.

Philanthropy emerges as a central theme in Chapter 9, offering a nuanced exploration of the impact of the Koch family's charitable initiatives on education, research, and societal well-being. The reader is encouraged to consider how these philanthropic endeavors have contributed to positive social change and the cultivation of intellectual resources.

The chapter also delves into the personal reflections of Charles Koch, his family, and those who have been part of the Koch Industries journey. Intimate anecdotes, interviews, and firsthand accounts provide a glimpse into the human side of a business magnate, offering readers a deeper understanding of the motivations, challenges, and triumphs that shaped Charles Koch's path.

In the concluding sections, the narrative transitions to a contemplation of continuations. Readers are encouraged to envision how the principles, values, and practices established by Charles Koch might influence future generations of business leaders, policymakers, and individuals passionate about making a positive impact on the world.

Chapter 9 serves as a bridge from the historical narrative to the ongoing conversation about influence, impact, and the responsibilities that come with success. As readers turn the final pages, they are left with a sense of the complexity, dynamism, and enduring nature of the Koch legacy—an invitation to contribute to the ongoing story of business mavericks shaping the course of history.

11

Epilogue: The Everlasting Echo

In this final chapter, the epilogue of "The Koch Chronicles: A Business Maverick's Journey to Influence and Impact," the narrative transcends the confines of the book, acknowledging that the story of Charles Koch and Koch Industries extends beyond the written words. It echoes in the corridors of history, the boardrooms of corporations, and the intricate tapestry of societal evolution.

The epilogue reflects on the enduring impact of Charles Koch's legacy, emphasizing that the true measure of influence and impact is often revealed in the echoes that resonate through time. Readers are invited to consider how the principles, innovations, and ideologies set forth by Charles Koch continue to shape the ever-evolving landscapes of business, politics, and societal values.

The narrative widens its lens to explore the global implications of the Koch legacy, contemplating how the maverick spirit of Charles Koch has influenced not only the American narrative but also the broader discourse on free-market principles, corporate responsibility, and the role of individuals in shaping the destiny of nations.

EPILOGUE: THE EVERLASTING ECHO

The epilogue delves into the reflections of scholars, thought leaders, and individuals whose lives have intersected with the Koch legacy. Their perspectives provide a mosaic of insights into the multifaceted impact of Charles Koch on the world, offering a nuanced understanding of the ways in which his journey has left an indelible mark on the collective consciousness.

As the final chapter unfolds, readers are encouraged to become active participants in the ongoing dialogue about influence, impact, and the responsibilities that accompany success. The epilogue becomes a bridge from the pages of a book to the broader narrative of human endeavor, prompting contemplation about the roles each individual plays in shaping the course of history.

Ultimately, the epilogue serves as a testament to the everlasting echo of Charles Koch's journey—a legacy that reverberates through the annals of business history and continues to inspire, challenge, and provoke thought in the minds of those who engage with the story. As readers close the book, they are left with a profound awareness that the echoes of influence and impact endure, creating ripples that extend far beyond the boundaries of time and ink.

12

The Unfinished Symphony

In this uncharted territory beyond the previous chapters, we find ourselves in the realm of the unknown—the unwritten, the unexplored, the future. Chapter 11 symbolizes the ongoing narrative, the ever-evolving symphony of influence and impact that transcends the confines of a structured book.

The narrative unfolds in the present and reaches into the future, contemplating the possibilities, challenges, and opportunities that lie ahead. It serves as a dynamic reflection on the continued legacy of Charles Koch, Koch Industries, and the broader themes woven into the chronicles.

Readers are invited to become active participants in the ongoing symphony, contributing their perspectives, ideas, and actions to the ever-expanding narrative. This chapter is an exploration of the collective influence that individuals and communities can exert, drawing inspiration from the principles and values instilled by Charles Koch.

The narrative navigates through the contemporary landscapes of business, politics, and societal values, encouraging readers to consider how the lessons learned from the Koch Chronicles can inform and shape their own journeys. The symphony unfolds in real-time, with each decision, innovation, and act of influence playing a part in the ongoing composition.

As readers engage with Chapter 11, they are prompted to contemplate their roles in the broader narrative of influence and impact. How do individuals contribute to the betterment of society? How do businesses navigate the delicate balance between success and responsibility? How does the political landscape evolve, and what role do individuals play in shaping its direction?

The chapter is an acknowledgment that the symphony is, and always will be, a work in progress—an unfinished composition with endless possibilities. The narrative extends an invitation for readers to embrace their roles as architects of influence, recognizing the profound impact that each individual can have on the world.

In the final notes of Chapter 11, readers are left with a sense of anticipation, recognizing that the symphony of influence and impact is a continuum— an ever-unfolding story that extends beyond the confines of a book. The legacy of Charles Koch becomes a source of inspiration for those who seek to contribute to the ongoing composition, leaving an indelible mark on the ever-changing tapestry of human history.

13

A Call to Action

As we draw the final curtain on "The Koch Chronicles: A Business Maverick's Journey to Influence and Impact," Chapter 12 emerges not as an epilogue but as a call to action—an invitation for readers to step beyond the pages of this narrative and into the realm of influence and impact in their own lives.

This chapter serves as a catalyst for reflection and engagement. It encourages readers to distill the insights gleaned from the journey of Charles Koch into actionable principles that can shape their individual and collective endeavors. The call to action resonates with the idea that the true legacy of any story lies not just in its telling but in the transformative potential it holds for those who engage with it.

The narrative becomes a springboard for contemplation: How can the principles of innovation, resilience, and ethical leadership espoused by Charles Koch be applied in readers' personal and professional spheres? What role can each individual play in fostering positive change within their communities? How can the spirit of influence and impact manifest in diverse fields and endeavors?

A CALL TO ACTION

Chapter 12 also serves as a platform for dialogue and collaboration. Readers are encouraged to engage with one another, sharing perspectives, ideas, and initiatives inspired by the Koch Chronicles. It becomes a hub for the exchange of insights, fostering a community of individuals committed to making a meaningful difference in the world.

In the spirit of Charles Koch's commitment to education, entrepreneurship, and the advancement of ideas, the chapter explores opportunities for lifelong learning and continuous improvement. It prompts readers to seek knowledge, embrace diversity of thought, and stay attuned to the evolving landscapes that shape our societies.

The call to action resonates not just on an individual level but extends to the collective. It invites readers to consider how they can contribute to the betterment of society, uphold ethical standards in their professional pursuits, and participate in shaping the narratives that influence our shared future.

As readers embark on their journeys beyond the final pages of this book, Chapter 12 becomes a compass—a guide for translating inspiration into action, for shaping personal legacies that echo with the principles of innovation, responsibility, and positive influence. The narrative, now a living testament, propels readers into the ever-unfolding story of their own influence and impact.

14

Summary

"The Koch Chronicles: A Business Maverick's Journey to Influence and Impact" is a comprehensive exploration of the life, career, and enduring legacy of Charles Koch, a pioneering figure in American business and politics. Spanning multiple chapters, the narrative delves into the early days of Koch Industries in Wichita, Kansas, tracing Charles Koch's trajectory from an ambitious entrepreneur to a formidable business magnate.

The chronicle unfolds through pivotal eras, each chapter illuminating different facets of Koch's journey. It navigates through the challenges and triumphs of Koch Industries, highlighting moments of innovation, diversification, and resilience. The narrative also explores the intersection of business and politics, as Charles Koch becomes a influential figure in shaping public discourse and policy discussions, advocating for libertarian principles and limited government.

The narrative does not shy away from complexities, delving into the tensions within the Koch family, the controversies surrounding the company's business practices, and the scrutiny of Koch's political activities. It examines the evolution of Charles Koch's management philosophy, known as "Market-Based Management," and its impact on Koch Industries.

SUMMARY

Chapters unfold as a tapestry of influence, impact, and transformation, examining how Koch Industries adapts to changing times, technological advancements, and global challenges. The narrative also extends beyond the business realm, exploring Koch's philanthropic initiatives, personal reflections, and the broader societal implications of the Koch legacy.

The concluding chapters transcend the confines of a traditional narrative, inviting readers to reflect on the ongoing impact of Charles Koch's legacy. The epilogue emphasizes the dynamic, ever-changing nature of influence, while subsequent chapters explore the unfinished symphony and the reader's role in the ongoing narrative.

In the final chapter, a call to action encourages readers to translate the insights gained from the Koch Chronicles into actionable principles. It prompts contemplation on how individuals can contribute to positive change in their communities, foster ethical leadership, and participate in shaping a collective future.

In summary, "The Koch Chronicles" weaves a rich and nuanced tapestry of Charles Koch's journey, exploring the intersections of business, politics, and societal impact. It invites readers to engage with the legacy, prompting reflection, dialogue, and a call to action that extends beyond the pages of the narrative.

www.ingramcontent.com/pod-product-compliance
Lightning Source LLC
LaVergne TN
LVHW010444070526
838199LV00066B/6182